P9-DBT-161

Masters of Music
THE WORLD'S GREATEST COMPOSERS

The Life and Times of

Ludwig van Beethoven

Mitchell Lane
PUBLISHERS

P.O. Box 196
Hockessin, Delaware 19707

Masters of Music

THE WORLD'S GREATEST COMPOSERS

Titles in the Series

The Life and Times of...

Visit us on the web: www.mitchelllane.com
Comments? email us: mitchelllane@mitchelllane.com

Masters of Music
THE WORLD'S GREATEST COMPOSERS

The Life and Times of
Ludwig van Beethoven

by Susan Zannos

Printing   3   4   5   6   7   8   9

Library of Congress Cataloging-in-Publication Data
Zannos, Susan.
        Ludwig van Beethoven/Susan Zannos.
            p. cm. — (Masters of Music. World's Greatest Composers)
        Summary: Discusses the life and career of the nineteenth century Austrian composer.
        Includes bibliographical references (p.) and index.
            ISBN 1-58415-190-0 (lib bdg.)
        1. Beethoven, Ludwig van, 1770-1827—Juvenile literature. 2. Composers—Austria—
        Biography—Juvenile literature. [1. Beethoven, Ludwig van, 1770-1827. 2. Composers.] I.
        Title. II. Series.
        M3930.B4 Z35 2003
        780'.92—dc21
                                                                                      2002153321

ABOUT THE AUTHOR: Susan Zannos has been a lifelong educator, having taught at all levels, from preschool to college, in Mexico, Greece, Italy, Russia, and Lithuania, as well as in the United States. She has published a mystery *Trust the Liar* (Walker and Co.) and *Human Types: Essence and the Enneagram* (Samuel Weiser). Her book, *Human Types*, was recently translated into Russian, and in 2003 Susan was invited to tour Russia and lecture about her book. Another book she wrote for young adults, *Careers in Education* (Mitchell Lane) was selected for the New York Public Library's "Books for the Teen Age 2003 List." She has written many books for children, including *Chester Carlson and the Development of Xerography* and *The Life and Times of Franz Joseph Haydn* (Mitchell Lane). Her great interest in classical composers inspired her to write this book. When not traveling, Susan lives in the Sierra Foothills of Northern California.

PHOTO CREDITS: Cover: SuperStock; p. 6 SuperStock; p. 9 Photo Researchers; p. 10 Corbis; p. 14 SuperStock; p. 17 SuperStock; p. 19 Corbis; p. 22 Corbis; p. 28 SuperStock; p. 30 Corbis; p. 32 Corbis; p. 34 Corbis; p. 38 Corbis; p. 40 AP Photos.

PUBLISHER'S NOTE: This story is based on the author's extensive research, which she believes to be accurate. Documentation of such research is contained on page 46.

The internet sites referenced in this book were all active as of the publication date of this book. Because of the fleeting nature of some web sites, the publisher cannot guarantee that they will all be active when you are reading this book.

Contents

The Life and Times of
Ludwig van Beethoven

by Susan Zannos

*   For Your Information

This portrait of Beethoven is by an unknown artist. It is now hanging in the Gesellschaft der Musikfreunde (Society of the Friends of Music) in Vienna, Austria.

New Pianist in Town

In November of 1792 Ludwig van Beethoven arrived in Vienna, the musical capital of Europe. He was 22 years old, short and thin. But in spite of being slender, he had powerful shoulders and arms, and strong hairy hands with stubby fingers. His head was large, with a broad forehead and bushy eyebrows. His hair was black and bristly. His eyes reflected his feelings: sometimes sad, sometimes flashing anger.

He was clumsy. He constantly bumped into, knocked over, and broke things. When he came to Vienna he got the name and address of a dancing master and even took a few lessons, but never did learn to dance in time to music. One lady wrote that he had "no exterior polish; on the contrary he was unmannerly in both demeanor and behavior." In short, Ludwig van Beethoven was an awkward young man who didn't know how to behave.

What he did know how to do was play the piano.

Beethoven had grown up in the much smaller town of Bonn, Germany. In addition to mastering his piano technique, he had also been an organist in the court there, played the viola in the orchestra and was already composing music.

Beethoven's name confused people. His grandfather came from Flanders where the prefix "van" was common. It did not show social class. In Vienna the prefix "von" meant that the person was a member of the nobility. People in Vienna assumed that the young man from Bonn was named Ludwig von Beethoven and was a member of the nobility. Actually his name was Ludwig van Beethoven and he was a commoner. When people made this mistake Ludwig did not correct them.

Young Beethoven had been invited to study with Franz Joseph Haydn, the most famous composer in Vienna. On his way back to Vienna after returning from a tour of London earlier in the year, the great composer had stopped briefly in Bonn. There he saw music composed by Beethoven. He said that he would accept Beethoven as his student if he came to Vienna. As it turned out, Beethoven was not grateful. He was stubborn and resented Haydn's criticism. He even started taking lessons with another teacher without telling Haydn.

Joseph Haydn was a kind man. He tried to help Beethoven. He wrote to the elector (a nobleman like an English duke) in Bonn asking him to send Beethoven more money to live on in Vienna. He also sent some of Beethoven's compositions. Haydn was embarrassed when he received the elector's reply: "The music of young Beethoven which you sent me I received with your letter. Since, however, this music, with the exception of the fugue, was composed and performed here in Bonn before he departed on his journey to Vienna, I cannot regard it as progress made in Vienna." Furthermore, it turned out that the elector was paying Beethoven much more than the young man had told Haydn about.

Haydn had planned to take Beethoven with him on his second trip to London. He changed his mind. However, he did arrange for another teacher to continue Ludwig's lessons in counterpoint. But

Joseph Haydn was not only a great composer, but also a kind and fatherly man who tried to help younger musicians. He agreed to teach Beethoven, but his efforts to help the young composer were not appreciated.

Beethoven's teachers all had problems with him. They said that he was so stubborn that he only learned through hard experience. He thought his teachers were jealous of him.

Awkward, shy, and unsure of himself, Beethoven often responded to people with anger. He thought people were insulting him when they were actually trying to help him. But the music-loving nobles of Vienna didn't care that Beethoven was hard to get along with. All they cared about was how he played the piano. And he played the piano brilliantly. His powerful playing style was very different from the gentle style of other pianists. He often made fun of these pianists and their style.

Beethoven's student Carl Czerny described his effect on audiences, "He knew how to produce such an effect upon every hearer that frequently not an eye remained dry, while many would break out into loud sobs. After ending an improvisation of this kind he would burst into loud laughter and banter his hearers on the emotion he had caused in them. 'You are fools!' he would say."

At this time the upper classes in Vienna loved pleasure. They wanted to forget the danger of war. The French Revolution in 1789

The people of Germany and Austria in the late 18th Century loved big parties and private concerts with which they attempted to forget the horrors of the French Revolution. This painting by Johann Franz Rousseau shows a masquerade ball at the Bonn Hoftheater in Bonn, Germany.

and the bloody reign of terror that followed frightened them. The death of their emperor, Joseph II, ended his policies of social justice. His successors, Leopold II and Francis I, persecuted anyone with liberal ideas. In order to forget these things, the Viennese competed with each other to see who could have the biggest parties and private concerts.

The piano, which had been developed early in the 18th Century, was the rage. There were over 300 pianists in Vienna. The children of the wealthy were all taking piano lessons from them. But in spite of the large number of pianists, very few were first-rate. Mozart had died in 1791. No one near his genius had appeared—until Beethoven arrived.

Ludwig wrote to his friend Frau von Breuning back in Bonn saying that he wanted to embarrass and have revenge on the Viennese pianists, whom he considered his enemies. During the next few years he met challengers for his position as the leading pianist in Vienna. The patrons of these musicians would set up piano-playing duels. The favorites would perform against each other, the way animals fight in an arena. In one of these duels the loser referred to Beethoven as "that young fellow who must be in league with the devil."

For his first three years in Vienna, Beethoven played mostly for aristocrats at their private concerts. After that his reputation spread and he made public appearances. The reviews were good. In 1796 he went on a tour to Prague, Dresden, Leipzig and Berlin. He performed at the Prussian court for the king, Friedrich Wilhelm II. The king gave Beethoven a gold snuffbox filled with gold coins.

Beethoven's student Czerny said that during this period of his youth, Beethoven "received all manner of support from our high aristocracy and enjoyed as much care and respect as ever fell to the lot of a young artist."

The nobility loved music. It was important to their social status to be known as patrons of an important artist. They gave Beethoven praise, money, and gifts. He later told his secretary and biographer, Anton Schindler, that these early years in Vienna were the happiest of his life.

Young Beethoven was spoiled, stubborn, and easily angered. Because of his talent as a virtuoso pianist he was supported by several noble patrons, sometimes living in their homes almost as a member of the family. This emotional support and feeling of belonging was something Beethoven longed for. It was something he had never had before. And he would never have it again. ◆

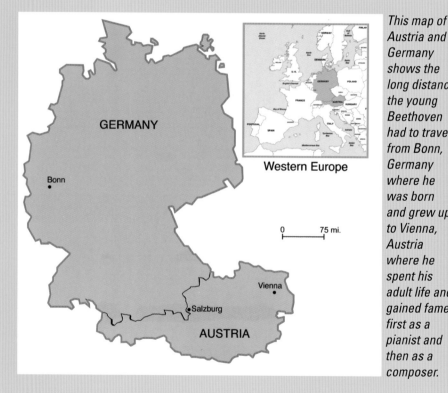

GERMANY

Bonn

Western Europe

0   75 mi.

Vienna

Salzburg

AUSTRIA

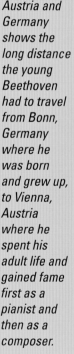

This map of Austria and Germany shows the long distance the young Beethoven had to travel from Bonn, Germany where he was born and grew up, to Vienna, Austria where he spent his adult life and gained fame first as a pianist and then as a composer.

THE
PIANO

The history of the piano may have begun several thousand years ago when a primitive hunter noticed that the string on his bow made a particular sound when he pulled it and let it go. Later, someone stretched strings of different lengths across an empty turtle shell. Each string made a distinctive note when it was plucked. That established the principle that vibrating strings made music.

The dulcimer, probably invented in Persia (modern-day Iran) in the 1st Century, uses the basic principle of the piano. Strings are stretched over a flat soundboard. The dulcimer player strikes the strings with light sticks that have blunt ends.

Early keyboard instruments were developed in the 14th and 15th Centuries. These had keys made of pieces of ivory, which were attached to objects that would hit or pluck the strings. The clavichord, first built around 1400, had a brass strip called a tangent that hit the strings. While similar in action to the piano, its tone was far too soft to be played in concerts. The next step was the harpsichord, which reached its peak during the period of Johann Sebastian Bach and George Frideric Handel. It was used both as a solo instrument and as an important part of the small orchestras of the 17th Century. It used rods that held a quill called a plectrum. When a key was pressed, the quill rose and plucked the string. Though it made a louder tone than the clavichord, there was no way of varying the strength of that tone.

But keyboard players wanted to be able to change the volume by direct finger action. So about the year 1709 an Italian harpsichord maker named Bartolomeo Cristofori constructed a new instrument that solved the problem. When the player struck a key, a leather-covered hammer would strike the string and cause it to vibrate. The sound level depended on how hard or softly the player struck the key.

Cristofori called his invention a "gravicembalo con piano e forte," which is Italian for "harpsichord with soft and loud." It soon became known as "piano e forte" (soft and loud), then pianoforte and finally plain "piano." So when you play the piano today you are literally playing "the soft."

This illustration is based on the famous portrait of Beethoven by Joseph Karl Steiler, painted in 1819. The artist captured the wild unruly hair and the intense gaze that sometimes frightened people. Beethoven gave Steiler several sittings for this portrait, which is now in the Walter Hinrichsen Collection in New York.

An Unhappy Childhood

L udwig van Beethoven was named for his grandfather who left Flanders (part of modern-day Belgium) to become a singer in Germany at the court of the elector of Cologne. The court was in the city of Bonn. Beethoven's grandfather married a woman who became an alcoholic. She was placed in a convent to be cared for by the nuns, leaving her husband to raise their only son, Johann.

Grandfather Ludwig van Beethoven became Kapellmeister, or music director, for the elector. His son Johann, father of the great composer, was also a singer and instrumentalist. Unfortunately Johann van Beethoven had his mother's disease: he also was an alcoholic. Grandfather Ludwig made sure that Johann was employed at court. Johann married a young widow, Maria Magdalena Keverich Leym, in 1767. His father objected to the marriage. After their son was born on December 16, 1770 and named after him, grandfather Ludwig supported the young family.

But young Ludwig's grandfather, the Kapellmeister, died when the boy was only three years old. The boy remembered him clearly, or claimed to, and idolized his memory. With the grandfather's

influence gone, Johann Beethoven proved unable to maintain the family dignity. For a while his father's reputation and memory were enough to keep Johann employed. But they were not enough to win him the position of Kapellmeister, which he thought he should have.

One result was that the boy had an unhappy childhood. His alcoholic father beat him and often forced his young son to play the clavier and the violin. Neighbors said that little Ludwig would be beaten or locked in the cellar if he refused to play. Or they would see him crying, standing on a footstool by the keyboard. It is surprising that he didn't grow up to hate music! His father may have hoped that he could force the boy to be a child prodigy like Wolfgang Mozart. Then the boy would make money. In 1778 Johann arranged young Ludwig's first public performance in Cologne. He lied about the boy's age, saying he was only six years old. Beethoven would remain confused about his age for most of his life.

Ludwig went to school in Bonn, but stayed for only a few years and did not learn very much. He did especially poorly in arithmetic and spelling. His schoolmates remembered him as dirty and poorly dressed, a shy boy who wanted to be left alone. The only times he seemed happy were when he could get away from town into the countryside.

But at least his music was going well. Johann hired other music teachers for his son. One of them lived with the Beethoven family and became Johann's drinking companion. The two men would drink in the taverns until after midnight, then come home and wake up the nine-year-old Ludwig. They would make the boy play all night. His mother could do little to help him. She was in poor health and busy with the younger children, his brothers Caspar Carl, born in 1774, and Nikolaus Johann, born in 1776. Four other children died in infancy.

In 1779 a musician named Christian Neefe arrived in Bonn. He was known for his Singspiele, a type of opera with spoken dialogue mixed with songs. Neefe became the organist for the elector in 1781. He recognized young Ludwig's talent and took him as a student. Neefe was very different from the boy's other teachers. He was well educated and had strong principles. He gave the boy the best music to study, music by Bach and Mozart. More importantly, he was kind.

Although Ludwig was not a child prodigy like Mozart, he became Neefe's assistant organist and played the harpsichord in the elector's orchestra at the age of 11. Neefe also showed him a lot of different types of music. Ludwig's first compositions were imitations of the court music common at that time. He wrote sonatas

Mozart was a child prodigy. This illustration by an unknown artist shows young Mozart at the piano with his father on the violin. His sister is on the other side of the piano.

for piano, three quartets for piano and stringed instruments, a trio for piano, violin, and cello and quite a few pieces for combinations of wind instruments since the elector liked to hear those while he was having dinner.

Soon afterward Ludwig began to earn some money giving music lessons to the children of a prominent family, the von Breunings. That family showed him kindness and remained his friends throughout his life.

The von Breunings were not only like a family for Beethoven, but they also helped to educate him. They had an extensive library and let him read the works of important writers and philosophers. Ludwig was attracted to the philosophy of Immanuel Kant, who wrote about the necessity for personal freedom. He almost worshipped the German poet Freidrich Schiller and soon wanted to set Schiller's poem "Ode to Joy" to music.

By 1787, he was so developed musically that the elector allowed him to take a trip to visit Vienna. But the trip was cut short after two weeks because Ludwig's mother became seriously ill. His father begged him to return home. Before leaving Vienna, Ludwig played for Mozart. When Mozart heard the boy improvise, he said, "Keep an eye on him: some day he will give the world something to talk about."

When he got back to Bonn, Ludwig found his mother dying. After her death he was left with his alcoholic father and two younger brothers to care for. He became the head of the household. When his father got into trouble with the police because of his drunkenness, the boy was able to take control of the family's finances. He went to the elector and asked to be given half of his father's salary. His request was granted.

Young Ludwig was now the main source of income for his father and younger brothers. Beethoven had many good friends among the musicians at the court, and many supporters among the nobility. In 1790, Emperor Joseph II died. A local poet wrote an ode that Beethoven set to music. It was called "The Funeral Cantata on the Death of Joseph II." But it was never performed. One of the court musicians later wrote, "We had all manner of protests over the difficult places—Beethoven asserted that each player must

In 1787, before he left Vienna to return home to his dying mother, Beethoven played for Mozart. When Mozart heard Beethoven improvise, he said, "Keep an eye on him: some day he will give the world something to talk about."

be able to perform his part correctly; we proved we couldn't, simply because all the figures were completely unusual—and so it was not performed at court."

The "Joseph Cantata" remained unknown until long after Beethoven's death. In 1884, the year that it was rediscovered, the composer Johannes Brahms wrote, "Even if there were no name on the title page, none other could be conjectured—it is Beethoven through and through! The beautiful and noble pathos, sublime in its feeling and imagination; the intensity, perhaps violent in its expression—all the characteristics which we may observe in and associate with his later works."

This cantata may have been among the compositions that Haydn saw during his stopover in Bonn that led to his invitation for the young man to join him in Vienna. The elector quickly granted him permission to go. One good friend, Count Waldstein, gave Beethoven letters of introduction to several of his friends there and told him that he would "receive Mozart's spirit from Haydn's hands."

Once again Ludwig van Beethoven set off for Vienna. This time he would stay. Soon after he left, his father died. Ludwig never returned to Bonn. Perhaps the painful memories of his childhood made him never want to go back.◀

MOZART

Wolfgang Amadeus Mozart was an amazing musical prodigy. He was born in Salzburg, Austria in January, 1756. When he was four years old, he began to play the harpsichord. He started to compose music when he was five. Leopold Mozart, Wolfgang's father, was a violinist at the court in Salzburg. He was also a composer and the author of a well-known work on methods of violin playing. He soon realized that teaching his son was a far more important task than creating his own music.

So Leopold decided to take the children on a series of musical tours. Wolfgang was six and his sister Nannerl was 11 when they began. They played at the most important royal courts of Europe. The boy's genius and charm won the hearts of the music-loving nobility.

In spite of the fame he achieved, young Mozart did not receive what his father most wanted for him: a secure position at a royal court. They returned to Salzburg in 1773, where Wolfgang was the principal composer and virtuoso at the court. He was paid little, and his work was not appreciated. He longed to escape to the brilliant world he had known when he was touring Europe.

In 1777 he again went on tour. By this time he was 21. He no longer was the great attraction he had been as a small child. He found that many musicians were jealous of his talent. Others thought he was a has-been, a one-time prodigy who had outgrown his fame. He returned again to Salzburg, which he hated more each time he went back.

In 1780, the city of Munich commissioned an opera from Mozart. The result was his first great theatrical work, *Idomeneo*. It premiered the following year and was a success. Mozart was confident enough to leave Salzburg and settle in Vienna where he continued to compose operas, symphonies, concertos and chamber music. He married, but he lived in poverty in spite of the success of his works. Without the patronage of the nobility, it was impossible for a composer to make money.

The great composer Joseph Haydn recognized Mozart's genius. The two became close friends, and Haydn did everything he could to help Mozart get an appointment at court. All efforts failed. In 1791, at the age of 35, Mozart died, weakened by diseases that were the result of his poverty. This great musical genius was buried in an unmarked pauper's grave.

From early childhood and throughout his life, Beethoven was truly happy only when he could be by himself in the countryside surrounded by the beauty of nature. While alone in the woods, he would fill his notebooks with musical ideas.

CHAPTER

3

Conflict

W hen Beethoven arrived in Vienna he rented a small attic room. But soon Prince Karl Lichnowsky, an important musical patron, invited Ludwig to live in one of his residences. Carl Czerny reported that the Prince treated Ludwig "as a friend and brother, and induced the entire nobility to support him."

This caused him both to be grateful and to struggle for independence. One time Beethoven overheard the prince telling his servant that if he and Beethoven should ring at the same time, the servant should go to Beethoven first. Beethoven immediately hired his own servant. Another time, when Beethoven was learning to ride, the prince offered him the use of his horses. Beethoven bought his own horse.

Sometimes Prince Lichnowsky was able to help the young composer without Beethoven knowing it. He secretly paid for the publication of Beethoven's first piano trios. Beethoven thought the profit he made—twice the amount of the salary he had made for a year in Bonn—came from the publisher.

The conflict between his need for support and his desire for independence caused many difficulties between Beethoven and his

patrons. He later told his biographer, Schindler, "They treated me like a grandson. The princess's affection would have made a glass shade to put over me, so that no unworthy person might touch or breathe upon me."

His problem was that he wanted to be accepted as a person. He wrote an angry letter to a friend saying, "Am I then nothing more than a music maker for yourself or the others?"

He felt that they were treating him like an object, the way a wealthy person today might buy a fancy stereo system. He didn't like it. Soon he began refusing to play the piano when he was asked to play. This stubbornness would cause serious quarrels between Beethoven and his patrons.

In spite of the conflicts he had over performances and living arrangements, Beethoven kept to a regular work schedule. He rose at dawn, had breakfast, and went to work at his desk until noon. Sometimes he took a short walk, but even then he took his note-book with him to write down his musical ideas. In the afternoon he took long walks around the city. In summer when he was at the estates of wealthy friends, he took walks in the countryside. In the evening he would meet friends at a tavern, go to the theater, or make music. He usually went to bed early, about ten o'clock, unless he had a creative idea that he continued to work on.

Wherever he was, at home or walking in the woods, in a tavern or sitting beside a stream, he filled his sketchbooks with ideas. He was happiest in natural surroundings. His creativity needed peace. He wrote in his diary, "Calm and liberty are the most precious of all possessions." In search of peace he constantly changed his dwellings. His desire for a home and family made him restless.

Beethoven's efforts to have a family included trying to get married. But he didn't have any luck. Two years after he arrived in Vienna, he proposed to a singer who had come from Bonn. She refused him, saying that he was "ugly and half-crazy." He fell in love over and over again, but the women either were already married or soon married someone else.

Many of Beethoven's conflicts with women, with his patrons, with other musicians, and with himself were the result of his high ideals. He had never known a happy family life. He imagined that it should be constantly joyful and loving. He thought people should always be good and kind. When real friends and real families didn't live up to his standards, he would become angry and fight with them. Then he would be angry with himself and feel guilty for what he had said and done. He would write letters of apology and remorse.

The conflicts in Beethoven's personal life did not harm his creativity during his first years in Vienna. He believed in the importance of his music. He believed that he had a mission to do good. He wrote to a friend that a person should try "to do good whenever one can, to love liberty above all else, never to deny the truth, even though it be before the throne."

This may sound like he believed in revolution. He did not. The good that he tried to do was creating beautiful music. The liberty he loved was to compose in his own way. The truth he was after was artistic, not political.

Haydn and Mozart had developed the forms of classical music to a very high level of excellence. Classical music emphasizes formal patterns. Beauty, order, and proportion are characteristics of classical music. Beethoven did not abandon these forms. He studied them carefully and used them. In his earliest compositions,

Beethoven was obviously learning from other composers and imitating their methods.

The music he wrote during his first years in Vienna was mostly piano music: piano sonatas, duo sonatas for the piano and one other instrument, and piano trios. He also wrote some string trios and quartets and worked on concertos and a symphony. These all followed the basic three and four movement sonata form. The sonata form is used in most classical instrumental music. It usually has a first movement in which two or more musical motifs are introduced and developed. Then there is a slow second movement, a fast third movement, and sometimes a fourth movement as well.

Even so, Beethoven was experimenting. Joseph Haydn advised him not to publish one of his piano trios. This made Beethoven angry. Haydn thought that it was too difficult for the audience to understand. Yet later this trio was most admired.

In the string quartets of his early Vienna period, Beethoven began experimenting even more. Sometimes he left out the slow movement. Sometimes he placed fast tempo sections in the middle of a slow movement. In his piano sonatas Beethoven moved even farther away from the traditional. In fact he called some of them, such as the famous Moonlight Sonata, "fantasy sonatas."

By the turn of the new century in 1800, Beethoven was 30 and starting to enter a new stage of musical development. He was taking the forms of classical music and adding the force of stirring emotional themes. He performed his first concert that year. The highlight was his First Symphony. While many people didn't understand it because it was so different from what they were used to, it was obvious that Beethoven had entered a new stage of musical development. But he was also starting to enter a new stage in his personal life. Ludwig van Beethoven was going deaf. ◆

THE
ENLIGHTENMENT

By the middle of the 18th Century, the feudal system in Europe was about to collapse. Feudalism is the general term used to describe the political and military system of western Europe during the Middle Ages. Feudalsim developed to meet the needs of its time. It was necessary after the Roman Empire was no longer able to protect people against the warring tribes that attacked from the north and east. The powerful landowning lord promised protection to the people who served him. Beneath him were other powerful nobles who provided soldiers for the army. And beneath the nobles were farmers, craftsmen, and servants.

For quite a few centuries this system worked fairly well. Then it didn't work so well. The powerful rulers spent enormous amounts of money on their palaces and pleasures, and didn't really need to protect the peasants from anyone but each other. The peasants still paid huge amounts of taxes, but got nothing much in return. In France this situation led to the French Revolution, which began in 1789 and continued its bloodshed and violence into the early 19th Century.

Elsewhere in Europe, particularly in Germany, the response to the social evils of the time was called the Enlightenment. Writers and philosophers and many members of the nobility claimed that human virtues could change society. Violent revolution was not necessary. The ideals of the Enlightenment were virtue, reason, freedom, progress, and brotherhood.

The philosopher who stated these ideals was Immanuel Kant. He wrote that "Morality is based upon the conception of man as a free agent." In other words, this "free man" could be trusted to act in the best interests of society.

Thinkers of the Enlightenment placed their hope in a ruler who would be wise and just. They did not think revolution was necessary. They saw the chaos that occurred in France when the common people took control. They thought it would be much better to have a ruler, as long as he was good and virtuous. In Austria and Germany, many thought that Emperor Joseph II was such a ruler. Even after he died in 1790, the ideals of the Enlightenment lived on in literature by writers like Schiller and Goethe.

This painting shows Beethoven at work in his living quarters. His student, Carl Czerny, who began his lessons when he was 10 years old, remembered that the composer's room "presented a most disorderly appearance: papers and articles of clothing were scattered about everywhere."

CHAPTER

Escape in Music

C arl Czerny was 10 years old when he began taking piano lessons with Ludwig van Beethoven in 1801. He later remembered his first visit to his teacher:

"The room presented a most disorderly appearance: papers and articles of clothing were scattered about everywhere. Beethoven himself recalled to me the picture in *Robinson Crusoe*, which I was reading at the time. His coal black hair bristled shaggily about his head. His beard—he had not shaved for several days—made the lower part of his already brown face still darker. I also noticed that he had cotton, which seemed to have been steeped in a yellowish liquid, in his ears."

The cotton in Beethoven's ears was the only outward sign of a ringing and buzzing that he had been aware of for several years. He went to many doctors, but none was able to help. In 1801 he wrote a long letter to a friend in Bonn telling him of his problem with his hearing: "For almost two years I have ceased to attend any social functions, just because I find it impossible to say to people: I am deaf—in my profession it is a terrible handicap—I cannot hear the high notes of instruments or voices."

Beethoven went on to say that people did not realize that he was hard of hearing because he had always been absent-minded. He avoided social gatherings and stayed alone most of the time.

The following year he wrote to his two brothers, "My misfortune is doubly painful to me because I am bound to be misunderstood; for me there can be no relaxation with my fellow men, no refined conversations, no mutual exchange of ideas. I must live almost alone, like one who has been banished."

Other letters he wrote to friends during that time were full of the suffering he felt at his loss of hearing. His longings for friendship and for participating in family life with his patrons were defeated by his need to conceal his deafness. He became more and more solitary. And people found him more and more strange and hard to get along with. In his isolation, Beethoven spent more and more of his time composing. He no longer performed as a piano virtuoso.

Napoleon Bonaparte brought order, stability, and military conquests to France after the bloodshed and suffering of the French Revolution. Later, his own ambition to conquer Russia defeated him and he was banished.

Despite his personal struggles, Beethoven was working on his Third Symphony, known as the "Eroica" (heroic) symphony. At this time the composer admired Napoleon Bonaparte. He thought the French general was brilliant and brave. Beethoven believed that Napoleon had the characteristics that the philosophers and poets of the Enlightenment wrote about.

But in 1804, just as Beethoven was finishing his symphony and preparing to dedicate it to Napoleon, he learned that Napoleon had declared himself Emperor of France. Beethoven was angry. He thought that Napoleon had betrayed the people who believed in him. The title page of the symphony called it "Grand Symphony Titled Bonaparte." Beethoven furiously scratched out the last two words. He rededicated it to one of his patrons.

It wasn't the only time that the influence of Napoleon Bonaparte would intrude on Beethoven. A new theater, Theater-an-der-Wien, had opened in Vienna in 1803. Its owner gave Beethoven the position of composer in residence. This meant he could conduct a concert there when he wanted to. It also meant he had to write an opera. That opera, *Fidelio*, is the story of a brave and faithful woman who rescues her innocent husband from prison. The story appealed to Beethoven's idealism.

Unfortunately, by the time the opera was produced in 1805, the French army was occupying Vienna after Napoleon had led a successful campaign into Austria. Most of the Viennese nobility had fled the city. There was only a small audience—mainly French officers. There were only three performances before it closed. *Fidelio* flopped again the following year. But Beethoven didn't give up on it. He made many changes and presented it for a third time in 1814. It was successful and *Fidelio* has been performed regularly since that time. ◈

During the French Revolution the common people rebelled against the nobility. King Louis XVI and his consort Marie Antoinette were beheaded. There were riots in the streets of Paris because the people were starving.

NAPOLEON FYInfo

Napoleon Bonaparte did more to spread the ideas of the French Revolution than any other leader. He was born on the Mediterranean island of Corsica in 1769 and went to school in France. After attending military school in Paris, he became an army officer at the age of 16. Four years later, in 1789, the French Revolution began.

In the years of turmoil that followed, Napoleon proved his genius leading the army. In 1795 he defended the new government from an angry mob in Paris. As head of the army in Italy he inspired the French soldiers with his bravery.

By 1799 the French people turned against their government. Napoleon became their leader in 1802. His success in war led to a brief period of peace. During this time he proved he was as skilled a statesman as he was as a general. His Code of Laws was so just that by the middle of the 20th Century over 70 countries used it as the basis for their own legal systems. The Code provided equality before the law, and did away with privileges of birth. It guaranteed freedom of religion and the separation of church and state.

The other countries of Europe did not like what was happening in France. The kings and nobles were afraid of the revolutionary ideas. The English, Austrians, Russians, Spanish and Italians attacked France, sometimes one at a time, sometimes joining forces. For several years Napoleon defeated them all.

Then in 1812 he invaded Russia with an army of about 500,000 men. They were defeated not by the Russian army but by Russia itself. The extremely cold weather and lack of food and shelter for the men and animals forced Napoleon to retreat.

After Napoleon's disaster in Russia, the other countries again attacked France. In 1814 Napoleon was forced to give up his power. He was sent into exile on the island of Elba, a small island between Corsica and Italy. Within a year he escaped, returned to France, raised an army and regained the throne. He surprised other countries by attacking first. But, then the British Duke of Wellington defeated him in the famous battle at Waterloo in June, 1815.

This time Napoleon was exiled to St. Helena, a tiny island in the middle of the South Atlantic Ocean more than 1,000 miles from the nearest land. He died there in May of 1821.

By the time Beethoven was thirty years old, he had begun to lose his hearing. As his deafness grew worse, he withdrew more and more from social contact. He ended his career as a virtuoso pianist and devoted his time to composing music.

CHAPTER

5

Vienna's Mad Genius

B eethoven's hearing grew steadily worse. Sometimes he would have periods when it seemed to get better. Then it would get worse again. After the first shock of this tragedy wore off, he would try to renew his friendships. In the summer of 1806 he went to the country estate of Prince Lichnowsky. But the difficulties he had with his patron continued. The prince asked Beethoven to play for some other guests. Beethoven refused, although the prince asked him repeatedly. The composer left the palace in the middle of the night and walked into town in the rain. He said, "There have been, and will be, thousands of princes; there is only one Beethoven."

In spite of the success of his music and the money he made from concerts and from publishers, Beethoven became more and more concerned about finances. He was not good at handling his money. He frequently had arguments with friends, publishers and even servants, accusing them of cheating him. He thought his life would be easier if he had an appointment at some court. He received an offer from Napoleon's brother Jerome, who had been created "King" of Westphalia, a German province not far from Bonn. Jerome offered him the position of court Kapellmeister. In spite of his negative feelings about Napoleon, he considered the offer. He wanted to leave Vienna. And it was a guaranteed income.

Three noble patrons, including Archduke Rudolph, brother to the emperor, guaranteed Beethoven a larger amount to stay in Vienna than Napoleon's brother would have paid him. So he stayed. The next few years would see some of his most impressive music, including the magnificent Fifth Piano Concerto, called the "Emperor." By 1812 Beethoven had produced eight symphonies, several concertos and an impressive amount of chamber music.

But soon afterward his output went into decline. There were two main reasons, one political and artistic, the other personal.

Napoleon's disastrous defeat in Russia and his final defeat at Waterloo removed him from power. With the threat of war removed, people's taste in art and music changed. They didn't want things that were serious. They wanted light-hearted tunes. Beethoven was out of fashion.

The personal reasons were probably even more important. His brothers, Caspar Carl and Nikolaus Johann, had moved to Vienna. Both had married, although Ludwig disapproved of their wives. His attempts to interfere with his brothers' lives created conflicts with them. He seemed to feel that the position he had once taken as a substitute father should entitle him to control their lives. They disagreed.

Perhaps his failure to have a family of his own made him envy his brothers' marriages. He had lost what may have been his most serious love. She was a mysterious woman known only as the "Immortal Beloved" from the love letter he wrote to her in 1812 but never mailed. His grief caused him to be depressed.

Beethoven had persuaded Caspar Carl to appoint him guardian of his son, Karl, in the event of his death. After Caspar Carl died from tuberculosis in 1815, Beethoven immediately tried to take his nine-year-old nephew away from his mother. The resulting legal and emotional conflicts continued for years. The boy was torn between his uncle and his mother. Beethoven insisted that his mother Joanna was an immoral woman unfit to even see her son. Sometimes the boy was in boarding school, and sometimes Beethoven decided to have the boy live with him in his disorderly rooms. Joanna asked the courts to restore her son to her. During the legal proceedings the court found out that Beethoven's pretense of being of noble birth was a lie. The case was then given to the court for commoners, where Joanna won custody.

Beethoven was obsessed with regaining custody of his nephew. By this time his deafness was complete. His behavior was more and more odd. He paid no attention to his clothing or to being clean. He would stomp about the streets of Vienna bellowing strange sounds. Children would follow him, laughing and making fun of him. Once the police arrested him for being a bum. Usually, however, he was left alone because in spite of his strange appearance and actions he still had friends in powerful positions. He was still Beethoven after all, even though during this period he was not producing any music.

In spite of being considered crazy, Beethoven managed to be again declared Karl's guardian in 1820. This calmed him somewhat. But it had the opposite effect on his nephew. Beethoven tried to control Karl completely. But this treatment made the boy miserable. At one point Karl ran away from school to be with his mother, but the police brought him back. Things came to a head in 1826. Beethoven wanted his nephew to attend a university. Karl wanted to join the army. So the unfortunate young man attempted suicide. This shocked Beethoven deeply. He agreed to let Karl join the army.

Beethoven is shown conducting one of his bold and original "Rasumowsky Quartets." The emotional fire of these string quartets stretched the forms of classical chamber music to their limits and foreshadowed the Romantic period in music.

CHAMBER
MUSIC

The term "chamber music" at first meant instrumental music that was not performed in a church, concert hall, or theater. It was played in smaller rooms as part of an evening's entertainment for the nobility. Today chamber music concerts may be held almost anywhere, and audiences consist of many types of people who love beautiful music.

Chamber music generally falls between music for a solo instrument and large-scale compositions for a full orchestra or chorus. It is regarded as serious music composed for two, three, four or even more instruments. Each instrument has its own part, and the parts are all on equal terms. Stringed instruments are particularly suited for chamber music, but there are also many fine compositions for wind instruments.

There are many types of chamber music. It might be a sonata for a piano with another instrument, frequently a violin, cello or wind instrument. The piano trio, which also includes a violin and a cello, has many famous compositions in its repertory. Trios of stringed instruments are also popular. Quartets are for four instruments, such as three stringed instruments with piano or four strings. Quintets, sextets, septets, octets, etc. are named for the number of instruments in the group.

Among these many types of chamber music, the most important is the string quartet, which consists of two violins, a viola, and a cello. Joseph Haydn is the composer who most influenced the development of the string quartet, writing more than 80 compositions. All of the great composers since his time have contributed to the repertory of chamber music.

Even though there are many professional chamber groups who give concerts, chamber music still has a private appeal as well. Friends who are amateur musicians often get together to enjoy playing chamber music in their own homes.

Many of Beethoven's works are performed today all over the world. His Ninth Symphony was recently added to the "Memory of the World" register. In this photograph, Justus Frantz bows after conducting a performance of Beethoven's Ninth Symphony by the Philharmonica of the Nations, the Ensemble Classique and the Kaunas State Choir, on Sunday, January 12, 2003 in Berlin, Germany.

CHAPTER
6

A Final Triumph

During Beethoven's darkest times, when he stumbled about the streets of Vienna like a ragged madman, people thought his career was over. Many of his friends and patrons had died. He no longer seemed to be producing music except for a few trivial pieces.

But appearances were wrong. He was creating what is generally regarded as his greatest single work. Known as the Ninth Symphony, it is much more difficult and massive than any of the preceding eight. In addition, he did something that was previously unheard of—using singers as part of a symphony. He set parts of Schiller's poem "Ode to Joy" to music, something he had thought about for more than 30 years. The choral section was included in the final movement of the Ninth Symphony.

But Beethoven was aware that the people of Vienna thought he was crazy. He was afraid his symphony would be rejected.

Making things even worse, there had only been time for two rehearsals. By this time he was totally deaf and could not hear how well the musicians performed.

So on May 7, 1824, Beethoven conducted the Ninth Symphony for its premiere performance in Vienna. When the last notes of the magnificent final movement came to an end, Beethoven stood on the stage with his back to the audience. One of the singers gently turned him around so he could see the audience. The applause was thunderous. Everyone was standing and cheering.

It was his final triumph. He became more and more with-drawn and died on March 26, 1827, less than three years later. There has been much speculation about the actual cause of the great composer's death. A young musician who visited Beethoven during his last days cut a small lock of his hair as a memento. In 2000, a chemical analysis of strands from this lock of Beethoven's hair revealed lead content 100 times greater than normal. Scientists currently believe lead poisoning from food and wine containers may have been the cause of his death.

After Beethoven died, twenty thousand people crowded into the square in front of his rooms and joined in the funeral procession. Vienna's suffering genius was at rest at last.

Beethoven seemed to be two different people. There was the man people observed, wild, sometimes angry and quarrelsome, disorganized, impulsive, often moving from place to place without ever completely unpacking before he moved again.

But inside this seeming madman was the composer, who was disciplined and painstaking. This inner artist was precise and a perfectionist, in some cases working on a piece of music over and over before he was satisfied with it.

Beethoven struggled in composing his music. He was not like Mozart, who seemed to make music effortlessly, as though it bubbled up in him naturally. Nor was he like Haydn, who composed

several pieces of music every month. Beethoven's notebooks show that he worked and re-worked his musical ideas.

Beethoven composed nine symphonies during his lifetime, while Mozart wrote more than 40 and Haydn wrote over 100! But the numbers don't tell the whole story. Beethoven's music was more complex, the movements far longer, the emotional content more profound than any that had been written before. He contrasted musical motifs in dramatic ways. His Fifth Symphony—perhaps the world's best-known symphony—begins with the familiar four notes that are startling, even threatening, like pounding on a heavy door at midnight. The second motif is in strong contrast. The tension between the two produces a complex emotion. And much of his music also expresses the joyous hope of freedom, peace and brotherhood.

During World War II, most of continental Europe lay under the yoke of Nazi tyranny. Every night, a powerful English radio station broadcast Beethoven's Fifth Symphony. Those first four notes—three short and one long—in Morse Code stand for V, or Victory. So even when things seemed darkest to those living under Nazi control, those broadcasts held out the hope for the eventual triumph of liberty.

And when the cruel wall that divided the city of Berlin was torn down in November, 1989 to end decades of dictatorial communist rule in Germany, there was no doubt about the music that would be played to commemorate the event. It was Beethoven's Ninth, and thousands of people of all ages jammed the concert hall to celebrate their new freedom. ◈

Selected Works

Orchestral Music: Beethoven wrote nine symphonies. Particularly well-loved are *Symphony No. 3*, called the *Eroica (Heroic); Symphony No. 5; Symphony No. 6*, called the *Pastoral*; and *Symphony No. 9*, the great choral symphony. Nine other orchestral works include his overtures to *Coriolanus, Leonore* (the first title given to his opera *Fidelio)*, and *Egmont* as well as *Prometheus* and *Wellington's Battle*.

Concertos: All five of Beethoven's piano concertos are often performed, but the *5th Piano Concerto*, called the *Emperor*, is usually acknowledged as the most brilliant. He also wrote one violin concerto and a concerto for piano trio with orchestra.

Piano Music: Beethoven's piano sonatas, such as the often-performed *Moonlight, Appassionata, Waldstein,* and *Hammerklavier* sonatas are favorites of concert pianists.

Chamber Music: Much of Beethoven's most successful chamber music was written for the piano with one or two other instruments. He wrote 10 sonatas for piano and violin, including *Spring* and *Ktreutzer*; five sonatas for piano and cello; and eight piano trios. He also wrote four string trios. Most famous are 16 string quartets including three *Rasumowsky Quartets*.

Choral Music: Beethoven wrote relatively little choral music, but his opera, *Fidelio* is a favorite. *Missa Solemnis* and *Mass in C Major* were also successful.

Complete Works: A complete index of Beethoven's compositions can be found in: Solomon, Maynard. *Beethoven*. New York: Schirmer Books, 1977.

Chronology

1770	born in Bonn, Germany on December 15
1778	first public performance in Cologne arranged by his father
1781	leaves public school; begins studying with Christian Neefe
1784	becomes Neefe's second organist at Bonn court
1787	travels to Vienna and plays for Mozart; mother dies
1789	becomes legally appointed head of family
1792	meets Joseph Haydn in Bonn; travels to Vienna; father dies
1795	performs his first concert in Vienna
1798	notices first symptoms of his deafness
1800	completes his First Symphony; first public concert
1803	becomes house composer at Theater-an-der-Wien
1805	first performance of his opera Fidelio
1809	granted annuity by wealthy patrons
1814	plays piano in public for last time
1816	becomes guardian of nephew Karl
1818	deafness becomes complete
1822	last effort at conducting
1824	wins acclaim with performance of Ninth Symphony
1826	nephew Karl attempts suicide
1827	Beethoven dies in Vienna, Austria on March 26

Timeline in History

1732	birth of George Washington
1750	Johann Sebastian Bach dies
1752	Benjamin Franklin invents lightning conductor
1755	Lisbon earthquake
1756	Seven Years' War between France and England begins (known as French and Indian War in American colonies)
1759	George Frideric Handel dies
1761	George III becomes King of England
1771	Luigi Galvani produces current electricity
1776	America declares independence from England
1780	Maria Theresa, Empress of Austria, dies
1781	Astronomer William Herschel discovers the planet Uranus
1783	American Revolution ends with the Paris Peace Treaty
1789	Fall of the Bastille in Paris begins the French Revolution
1791	Mozart dies
1793	French King Louis XVI and Queen Marie Antoinette beheaded
1797	Composer Franz Schubert is born
1799	George Washington dies
1800	Alessandro Volta develops electric battery
1804	Napoleon declared Emperor of France
1809	Composer Joseph Haydn dies
1812	United States declares war on Britain
1815	Wellington defeats Napoleon at Waterloo
1820	King George III of England dies
1824	King Louis XVIII of France dies
1826	Thomas Jefferson and John Adams, signers of the U.S. Declaration of Independence, both die on July 4—the document's 50 anniversary
1837	Victoria becomes Queen of England and begins 64-year rule
1848	gold is discovered in California.

For Further Reading

For Young Adults:

Lockwood, Lewis. *Beethoven: The Music and the Life.* New York: W.W. Norton & Co., 2002.

Tames, Richard. *Ludwig van Beethoven.* New York: Franklin Watts, 1991.

Vernon, Roland. *Introducing Beethoven.* Parsippany, NJ: Silver Burdett Press, 1996.

On the Internet:

Beethoven: The Immortal: http://www.lucare.com/immortal/bio.html

The Beethoven Reference Site: http://www.kingsbarn.freeserve.co.uk

Classical Music Pages: Ludwig van Beethoven: http://w3.rz-berlin.mpg.de/cmp/beethoven.html

Biography of Ludwig van Beethoven: http://top-biography.com/9082-Beethoven/life1.htm

Biography of Beethoven: http://classicalmus.hispeed.com/articles/beethoven.html

Biography of Carl Czerny: http://classicalmus.hispeed.com/czerny

On Video and DVD:

Dramatization of Beethoven biography: *Immortal Beloved.* A film by Bernard Rose, starring Gary Oldman. Columbia Pictures

Works Consulted:

Cooper, Barry. *Beethoven.* New York: Oxford University Press, 2001.

Matthews, Denis. *Beethoven.* New York: Vintage Books, 1988.

Schindler, Anton F. *The Life of Beethoven.* Trans. Ignace Moscheles. Mattapan, MA: Gamut Music Company, 1966.

Solomon, Maynard. *Beethoven.* New York: Schirmer Books, 1977.

Stanley, Glenn. *The Cambridge Companion to Beethoven.* New York: Cambridge University Press, 2000.

Valentin, Erich. *Beethoven, A Pictorial Biography.* New York: Viking Press, 1960.

Note to Researchers:

Upon his death, Beethoven left as rich a mass of documentary material as any composer in history. Among this material are scores of works, both published and unpublished, sketchbooks, and his Conversation Books, containing uncensored personal conversations between the deaf composer and his associates during his final decade. Among his effects were also found a diary he kept from 1812-18 and his passionate letter to an unidentified woman ("Immortal Beloved"). From this material, much has been learned about Beethoven. His biography by his former assistant Anton Schindler was much translated and used for years as the reliable conception of Beethoven. Some scholars in the twentieth century have found Schindler's portrait of Beethoven to be biased and self-serving and they have set about to correct some misconceptions. We have not relied on any one definitive source for this book, but have, in fact, sought out what is believed to be the most accurate account by present-day standards.

Glossary

cantata (kan-TA-ta) - instrumental and vocal composition, with both solo and choral parts

clavier (KLAV-ee-ur) - keyboard instrument with strings

concerto (kon-CHAIR-toh) - composition for orchestra featuring one (or more) dominant solo instrument(s)

counterpoint (KOWN-ter-poynt) - the art of plural melody where multiple melodies are interwoven

Elector (ee-LEK-tur) - German nobleman, comparable to an English duke

fugue (fewg) - musical composition in which various parts, or voices, are woven together according to strict rules of counterpoint

harpsichord (HARP-see-kord) - stringed keyboard instrument that uses a quill to pluck its strings

improvise (IMP-row-vize) - play music composed on the spot, rather than using sheet music or memory

kapellmeister (kuh-PEL-my-stur) - music director at an aristocratic court

opera (OP-ruh) - drama set to music, with most (if not all) of the dialogue sung

patron (PAY-trun) - person who supports an artist, usually financially

prodigy (PRAH-di-gee) - extraordinary person, particularly an unusually talented child

Singspiele (SING-speel) - musical drama in which arias alternate with dialogue

sonata (suh-NOT-uh) - composition for one or two instruments, usually in three or four movements of contrasting tempos

symphony (SIM-fun-ee) - elaborate instrumental composition for a full orchestra

virtuoso (vir-chew-OH-so) – someone who has great skill in playing a musical instrument

Index